Young Learner's

Step by Step

Young Learner Publications®
G-1A Rattan Jyoti, 18 Rajendra Place, New Delhi- 110 008 (INDIA)
Tel: 25750801, 25820556, 25755559 Fax: 91-11-25764396
Website: www.goodwillpublishinghouse.com
E-mail: gph.ylp@goodwillpublishinghouse.com
goodwillpub@gmail.com

Scribbling

Before you start drawing
it is very important that you learn the basics.
Scribbling is the first step towards making any sketches
as it improves your hand movements and familiarises you
with the flow of the lead pencil. Practise the scribbles
given below without lifting the lead pencil
off the paper.

Practise the scribbles in the boxes provided alongside.

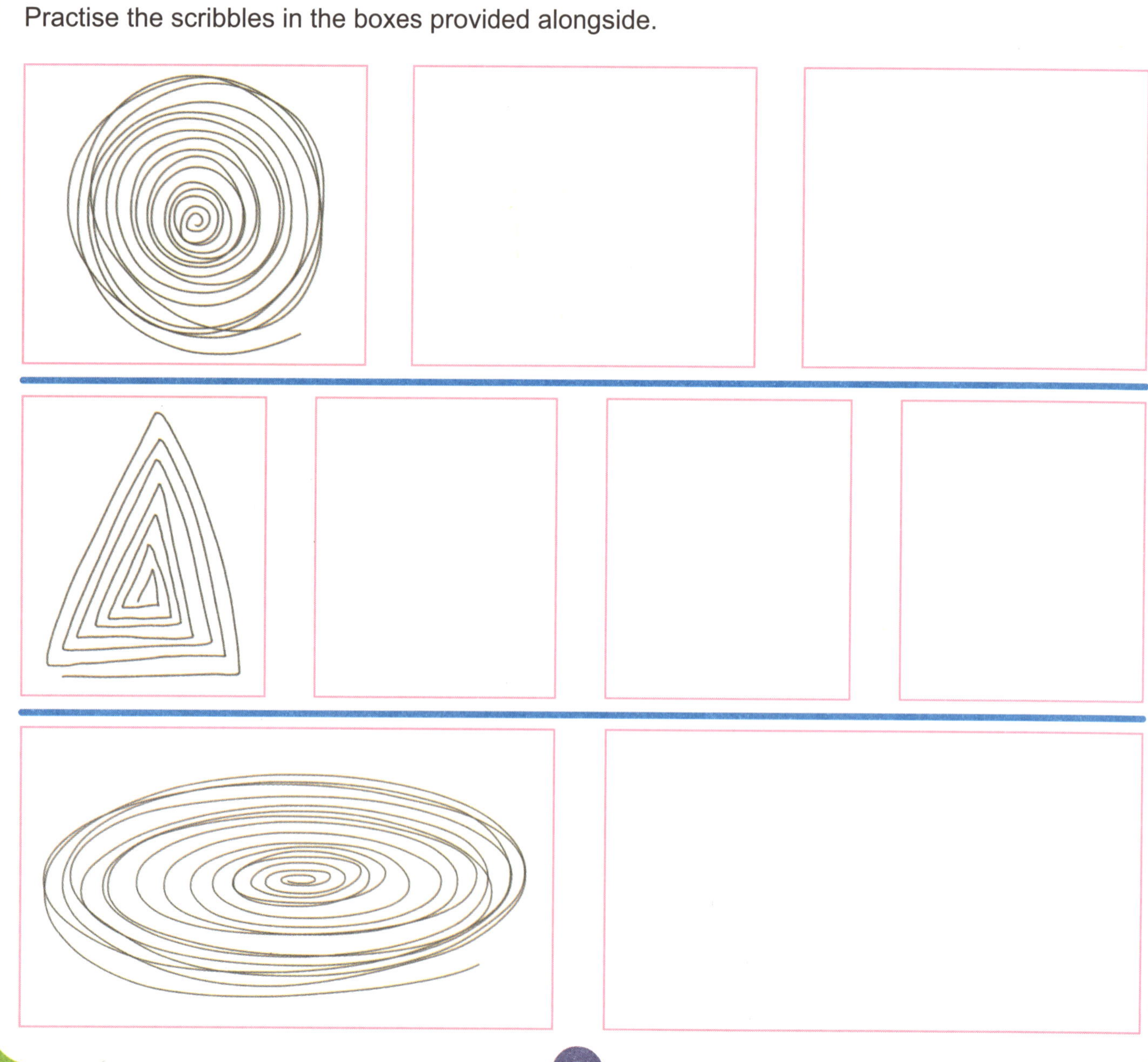

Practise the scribbles in the boxes provided alongside.

For teachers and parents: Besides this exercise, encourage the children to practise scribbling in their sketchbooks.

Fruit Scribbles

Now, using the scribbling technique we shall learn to draw simple fruit scribbles. You only have to draw the outer shape of each fruit. Remember not to lift the pencil off the paper.

Practise the fruit scribbles in the boxes provided alongside.

Apple

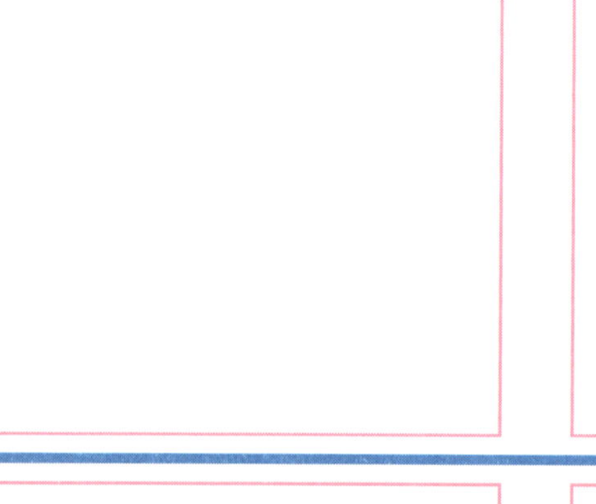

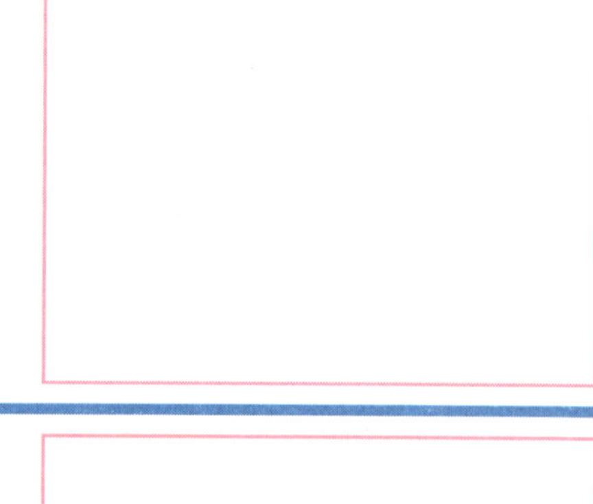

Grapes

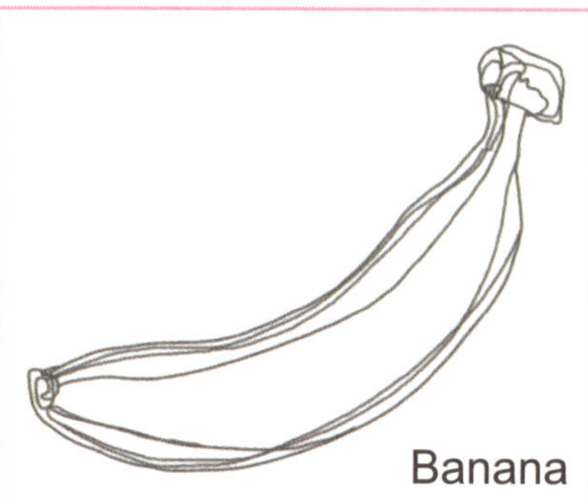

Banana

For teachers and parents: Besides the fruits given in the exercise, encourage the children to practise scribbling other fruits in their sketchbooks.

Patterns

We will practise making different patterns in this exercise before we start drawing anything further. Patterns are very important for perfecting your hand movements in different directions. It also helps you to draw all kinds of shapes.

Copy the patterns in the boxes given below.

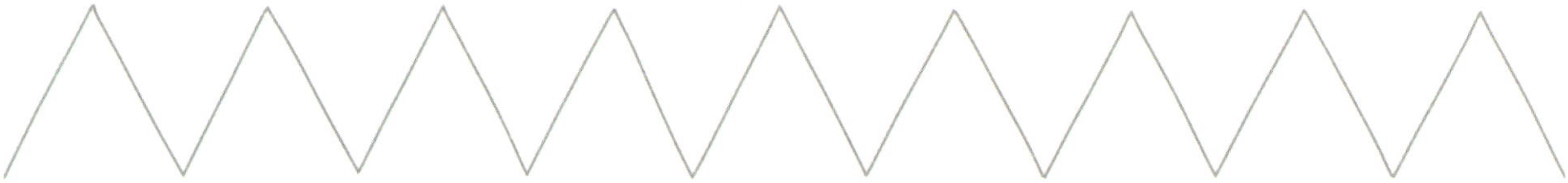

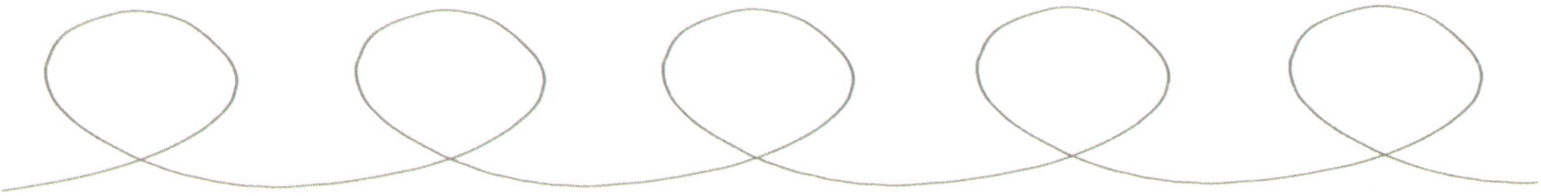

For teachers and parents: Besides this exercise, encourage the children to practise the patterns as much as possible in their sketchbooks.

Shapes

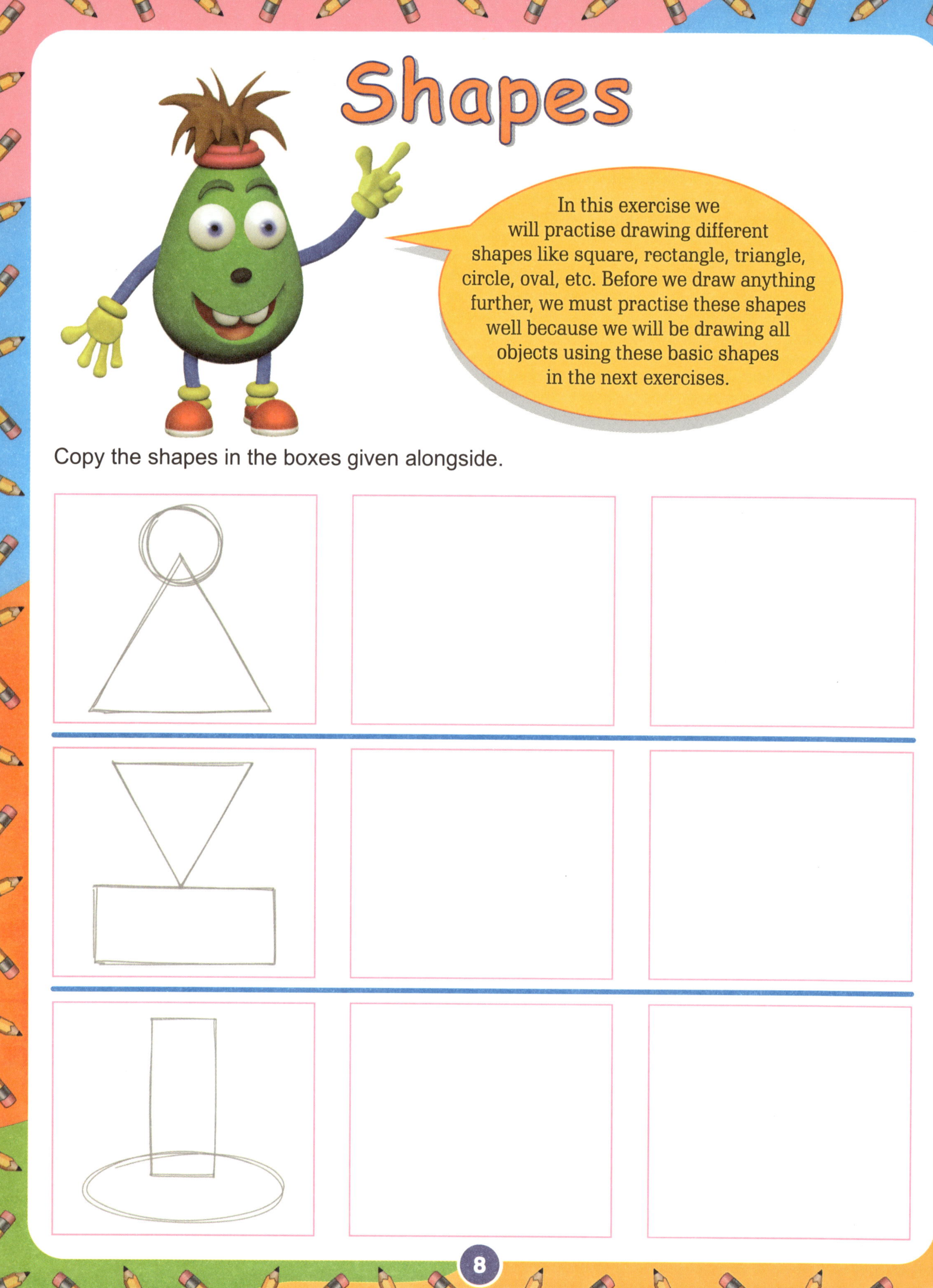

Copy the shapes in the boxes given alongside.

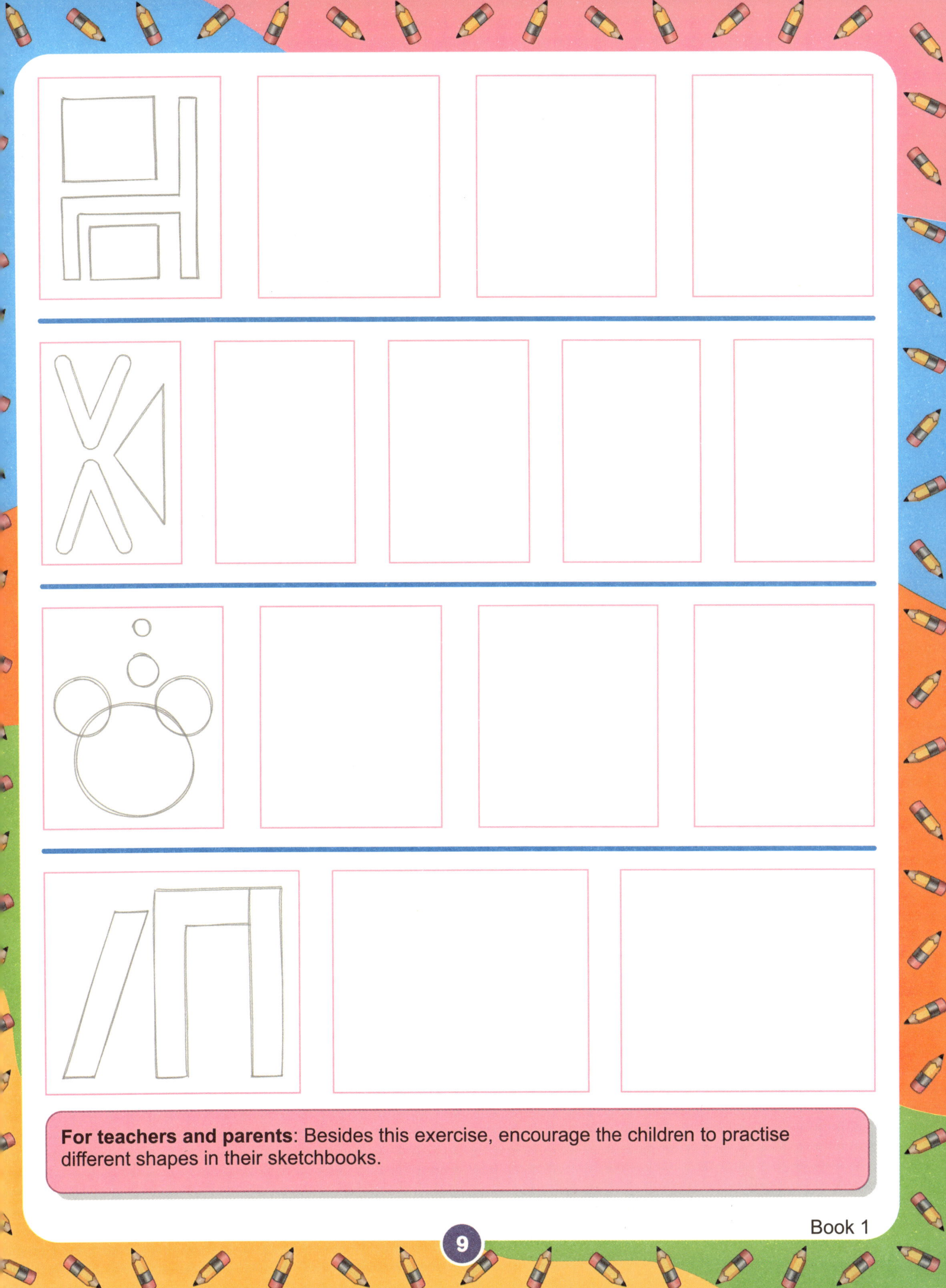

For teachers and parents: Besides this exercise, encourage the children to practise different shapes in their sketchbooks.

Drawing with Shapes

In this exercise, we will use different shapes for making objects found around us. Forming proper shapes is important to achieve right proportions in an object you are drawing. We choose the shapes according to the object we have to draw.

Follow each step of drawing the school bus carefully. Draw with the lead pencil in the boxes given alongside and colour with crayons.

Follow each step of drawing the car and tractor carefully. Draw with the lead pencil in the boxes given below and colour with crayons.

1 2 3

1 2 3

1 2 3

1 2 3

Follow each step of drawing the steam engine and ship carefully. Draw with the lead pencil in the boxes given below and colour with crayons.

1	2	3

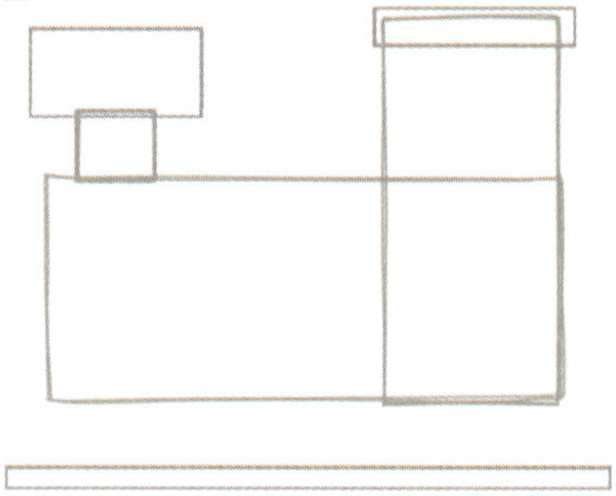

1	2	3

1	2	3

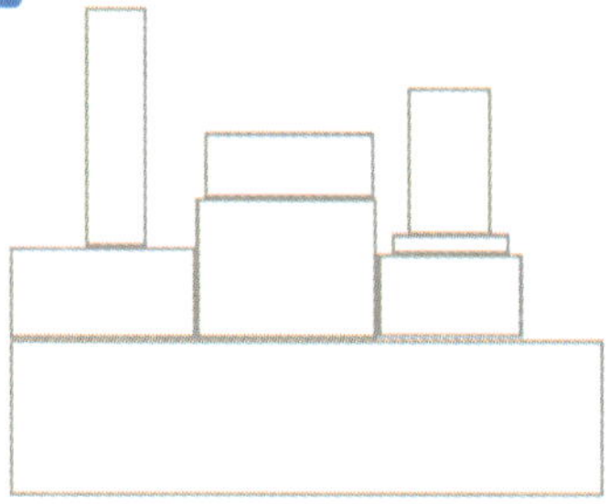

1	2	3

Follow each step of drawing the boat and house carefully. Draw with the lead pencil in the boxes given below and colour with crayons.

1	2	3
1	2	3

1	2	3
1	2	3

Follow each step of drawing the airplane and helicopter carefully. Draw with the lead pencil in the boxes given below and colour with crayons.

1	2	3

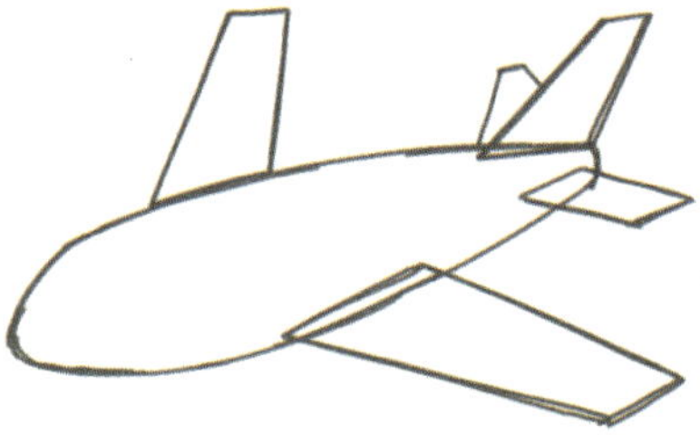

1	2	3

1	2	3

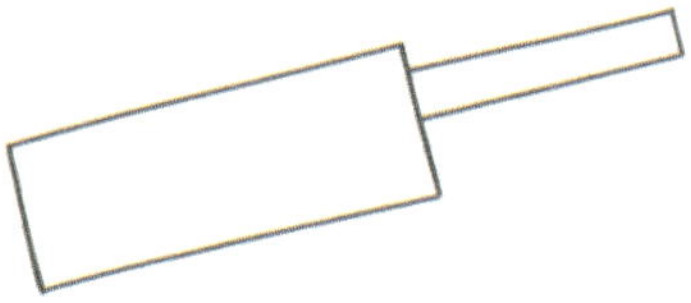

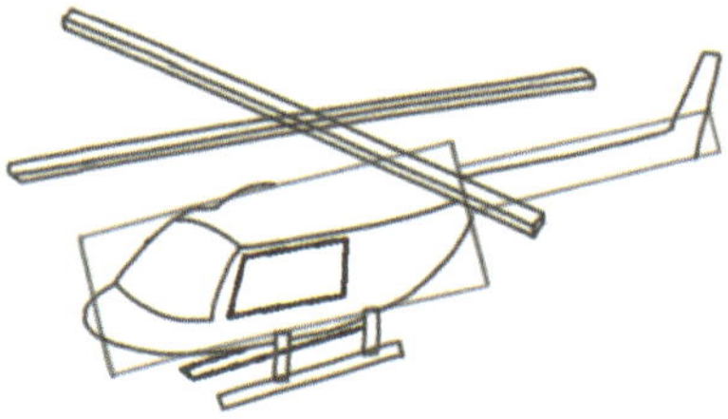

1	2	3

Follow each step of drawing the bicycle and horse carriage carefully. Draw with the lead pencil in the boxes given alongside and colour with crayons.

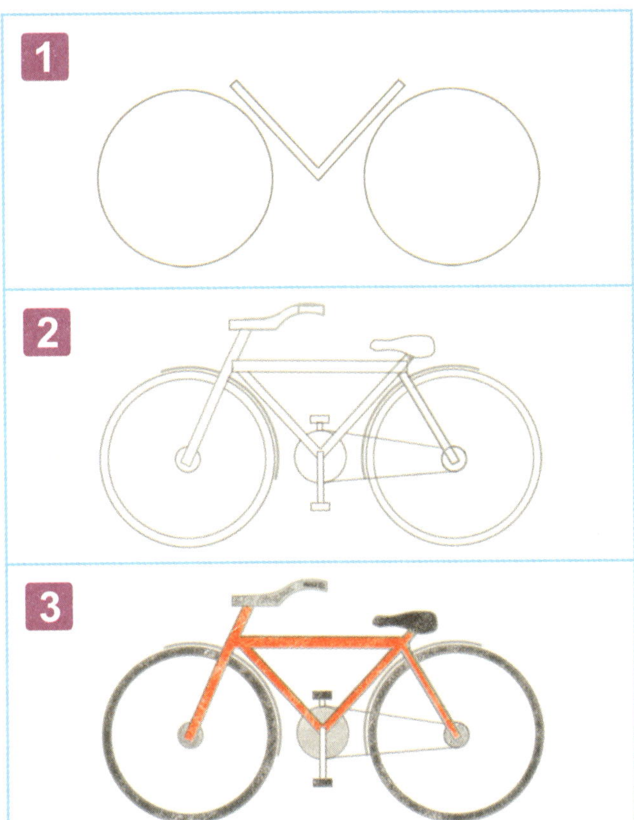

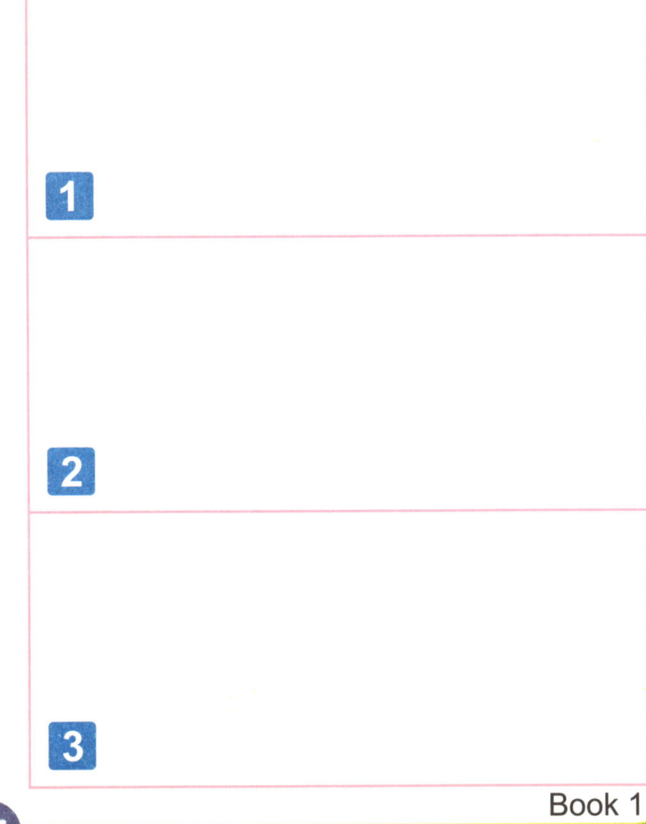

Follow each step of drawing the flower and trees carefully. Draw with the lead pencil in the boxes given alongside and colour with crayons.